AF241450

For the lovers

# honeytrap

poetry
by
k. wildside

ISBN: 978-1-9994593-0-7

Written by K. Wildside @kwildside
Design by Cheryl Payette

I was travelling north
To a cold and dark discord

But everything went south
When I saw your face in the crowd

So my heart went west
Wanting to kiss you till death

And watch the sun set east

You would be all I need

k. wildside

That sweet veil
You laid over me

Made from our tale
In your eyes

Will help me sleep again tonight

If I lean on your shoulder

Will you make it all better

Or will you turn it colder

I feel like my heart is running

To catch you when you are away
And to love you when you stay

I feel like my heart is beating

All the walls around me
And the ghosts in my sleep

I feel like my heart is wearing

Your

Name

I guess I hate the sun
For when it comes
Is when you leave
My mind
Is when we run out of time

At night is where I keep you safe
At night

Is when you are mine

k. wildside

I ran out of eyes for you
Walking slowly to healing

Out of spite
I will be standing

On your shoulders

Like you have been doing

Watching me suffer

I am still waiting on you
To knock at my heart
Late at night
To bring back what you teared apart
All the tiny little pieces

So essential to my life

k. wildside

There is still flowers
To be gathered
And ready to bloom
Inside of you

There is no telling
In the mirrors
If our hands will be holding

There is no telling
In the shadows
If we will be shining

k. wildside

So sorry I had to cheat on you
My love, my only
But I had to touch the skin
Of what it could be

My dear romance
So sorry I took the chance
It wasn't like the movies
It wasn't like the sad songs
Nothing felt like we belong

But at least
Now I know
To listen to your whispers
And your soft words

She is a special kind
She sees the fireworks at noon
The birds sing at midnight

She can feel before the touch
And look
With her eyes wide shut

She is a special kind
Her love runs through time

And right through mine

k. wildside

You are my motion picture
It is like you have read
My scenarios
And played it better

It is by your lips
That I want to cry
From all the joys
I feel inside

I need you to taste
How you make me feel

Alive

k. wildside

I will carry
Your heavy heart
And your clouded mind
On my shoulder

So you can breathe
And have faith
In your smile again

I am a secondhand love

Ready to be thrift away

k. wildside

I am used to feel cold
Not do as I am told

And there

You stepped in my life
Quite overnight

So my offer is

Walk with me slowly
Talk to me simply

And eventually

We will be

As if I could break your spell
As if
As if I was able

Impossible

k. wildside

25

I wanted to write you
A love letter
But honey you are
All the letters
Stitched together

You are all the words
My mind ever wondered
Anything I would lay
On this paper
Would not be enough

You are all of them
And somehow

Better

Sliding between the corners
Of your smile
Sure is a wild
Ride

k. wildside

The honeymoon
It revolves around us

She will kiss in loop
While we love till dust

Covering us of sugar
Now we taste like

Forever

Can you ask your name, politely
To come lay on my tongue
Can it stay there, eternally
At least, for more than a song

I want to taste the purity
Of a love unstained
And how lovely it feels
To be driven crazy

k. wildside

Handle with care
Do not stare
Do not scream
More fragile that it seems

Be brave
Stop being safe
Break away from your cage
Be brave

k. wildside

We start to learn
And start to lean
Towards each other

It starts to burn
Now can't be seen
Without each other

You are my pages
You are my words

You are who I have been looking for
For ages

You are my girl

k. wildside

It all happened so quick
That I couldn't breathe
It's like you stole the air
Only to wrap it up
And give it back to me

Out of the blue
You came
And got me out of mine

It had to be you
Because everyone is the same
And fairytales were lying

k. wildside

Let this heart piece go
A new one is gonna grow

And soon enough

You will feel it's glow

It is in her bed sheets
With her eyes closed
That she can achived
The life she wants to lead
A life that she chose

k. wildside




She dreams to be a star
Because just like her
Death kissed her heart
But still shines through the weather

All she wanted was a sky
Crystal clear and bright
But she wouldn't take mine

The colors made her jealous

I said they're painted after you
She smiled a little nervous

And I pointed at the moon

k. wildside

She put the flowers there
Where she could see them
And feel the love vanishing
With a single stare

I still feel the breath
Between these four letters
It's not the end yet
I can hear your whisper

Stay alive
Or I will need you to lie

k. wildside

It is a snowflake
Kind of relationship
We don't get too close
Or it might evaporate

And again I'm sitting here
Just across from my thoughts

So beautiful and light
They got me wondering
What it would be like

If we could turn tables

k. wildside

Grab this moment by the hand
Bring it up to the sky
Let it shine like a star
So no matter when
No matter where we are
We can remember why

It will always be

You and I

Saw a glance of you real quick
As my heart burns on the sand
Never felt a warmth like this
It all burned to ashes

As I try to comprehend

You are my last drop
Before it shatters
I have had enough

This glass heart
Can't take anymore lost

I have a heart to hide
I have my pride left to die

Don't know if I should seek
And let my lust lead

This is me honoring my pledge
This is you standing over the ledge

I want to be one of yours
But just a few pages

Enough to remember our faces
When we are not anymore

Because too much
Is nothing but greed

And not what love is for

You're laying there
Right beside me
And I'm looking at you
Feeling empty

I was counting on you
To show me how it is

I guess I was wrong
Because it still feels

Like I'm alone

k. wildside

Well I think today
Was one hell of a day

You brought me to the seventh
Without having any words to say

A look, a smile

And a little something

Am I making sense
Or my loving can't
Seem to understand
How to hold your hand

k. wildside

Laying there in your bed
Dreaming of fresh air

In your queen sized head

Let's sleep under
Both of our hearts
Let them jet us
To the love in the stars

k. wildside

Don't cry for what you have lost<br>
For it all makes sense<br>
Once you give it a thought

Smile for the joys it brought

Goodbye to the tears you dropped

This time it's on my term
I learned
What needed to be learned
And I burned
Everything you touched

Now
I'll stay friends with your ghost
So I know better
Than being a lonely lover

k. wildside

55

Cross my heart
See me on the other side
Hope I will see you there

Look both ways
Be careful
It is quite dark

My past shut all the lights

You wear me out
Like your favorite t-shirt

Until the last thread
Gets off your skin

k. wildside

Only in the summer
That my heart burns
Into a thousand lovers

Only in the summer
That my head learns
How to live lighter

We were never just lovers
Never just a single word

We were what people heard about
What everyone is looking for

We were golden in the crowd
Our heart was just to die for

k. wildside

I remember when
I was your sometimes
Somedays your maybe

I remember when
I wished you were mine
Always here with me

Then we let the night
Take our beautiful shine
But today I feel
Like the stars are aligned

k. wildside

When the here and now gets too much
There's always the back and then
Calling the lost

Where the home once was
Where there was an ounce of sense

Because at this moment
All and nothing

Is everything

Dripping through my hands

Only by keeping them shut
That you can find what you have not

Let it guide you through its path
Bring you heartbeats at last

It will hide at plain sight
So keep them shut

And let it make it right

k. wildside

So you let me watch
My demise
The premise from my own eyes

As the words you write
Wished they were mine

I see them laid down
Hoping not to drown
And be washed away

Her hair
Felt like a secret
That could strangle
The best
Of lovers
And angels

k. wildside



To the feelings
I don't want to feel

I lay you all on this page
So you can manage to kill

My heart shaped maze

You say you don't want to hurt me
But the hurting starts
Quite instantly

Those words are at war
So it makes you

My enemy

k. wildside

I recall it was midnight
Both alone in sight

We got into a heartcrash

Where our lives changed
Forever

Just like that

You don't know how to show it
But you hold my hand
You don't know how to say it
But you write with heart intent

Sometimes you're playing distant
Sometimes you want to wear my scent

But all I need
Is one of you

k. wildside

It's from our messy bed
Where our love is spread
That our sheets stare
Right into our head

Wrapping us with care
All we need to stay in love

I need you here
Closest to my tears

So you can have a taste
Of why my heart hates

You

k. wildside

I hate you so much
Now that I need your touch

You're bad for my breathing
Essential for my healing

Sound good on my heartstrings

Gold your eyes
Black your hair

You're the only sky
Your limit in the air

k. wildside

This I will say
Do not chase your dreams

Let the dream do the chasing
The one that is always in the way

When it calls your name
You rise
That one who brings you pain
Should be the only by your side

I know your letters are unsung
But I promise that one day

Someone will come along
And make everything ok

k. wildside

It left through the back door
Running scared
It couldn't take this anymore
No one dared to care

I caught you red handed
Playing with my love

Everything was turning blue

It's when I knew
You weren't the one

Who would go to the moon

Or bring me the sun

k. wildside

I feel like we meet questions
More than kissing answers
Dating self-doubts
More than loving a person

Only you can blue your sky
Only them can wrong your night

No one but you can make it right

You live inside yourself
Where you find peace and smiles
Step out of your realm
And find doubts and lies

The streets are wild
But inside your run free

No need to please
No need to hide

You make yourself happy
And that's all that you need

k. wildside

Don't shape your mind with troubles
They don't see in the clear

Keep your eyes high from rumbles
Keep your heart away from the tears

Walk your head in the light
Until they are out of sight

You were a passenger
One who crossed my heart

For a while

Your steps were a piece of art
Your touch was my life saver

k. wildside

You want to be today
So it is tomorrow
But you only breathe for now
So you drown in your sorrows

Rest your kiss on my chest
Make it live on your sweetness

Keep me alive
Out of my loneliness

Well,

At least just for the night

k. wildside

There is miles and miles of roads
In between our two loved souls

But the feelings in our words

Is what brings us close

I will let her wild

Her hair out of style
And her words
Free as a bird

Because that's how I love her
That's why I fell on this earth

k. wildside

Her home is a skinny storm
That love taught her to control

Now she lives on her own

Battling her mind, body and soul

Lend me that piece of you
The one that feels like you

I want to know where you've been
When I wasn't touching your skin

k. wildside

I agree
All roads lead to Rome
But nothing is built in a day

Patience, my love
We will find our way home

You like to keep it blurred
Not seeking for a cure

That's how you learned to love

That's how you don't get hurt

k. wildside

She said it was dead
She said it was dark blue and empty red

But she still wanted it to be held

Like nothing ever happened
Like it was still beating

Before the words were said

You cross the street
Like you crossed your heart

Eyes shut
And quiet

As long as you can't see
It can't tear you apart

I paint everything
With insecurities

Keeping everything blurred
I am my own casualty

It has nothing to do with us

So stay where you are

And I will run straight to you

Sometimes to love is to be a stranger

k. wildside

Once she read
Find what you love and let it kill you
It stuck in her head
It's what she needed to do

She wrote his words on her neck
It was her life sentence
With a smile she went to rest
Knowing it's how it's supposed to end

Nothing could stand between her and the moon
This space is hers to be safe and dazed into
She has all the time and all the warmth to bloom
All of this and more until a star shined through

With the thought of it just flying by
She flew along for a short time
But the star stayed in sight
And all she missed was her space to hide

So she fell fast from the sky
Leaving it alone to shine bright

k. wildside

You played your finger on my bones
She said I just want to be alone
Your melody stained my mind
She said I don't want to waste your time

He said she said all the same
But I dazed into snake eyes

She turned her back forgot my name
All she said were heart shaped lies

I hope we can lay there in silence
And be comfortable in the moment
Just holding hands
Knowing where we stand

Our smiles could do the talking
And the sky could watch us

Falling

k. wildside

97

I'm on strike
Until my heart bleeds dry

It shattered into four letters

I don't know

If someone could possibly

Bring them back

Together

So fast she felt it all at once
Never expected this much
Her blood straight to her head
In a such a rush

So fast she felt it all at once
But the stars weren't aligned
She had too much on her mind
And had water in her lungs

So fast she had to let it go
So that maybe once again
Their hearts would glow
And shine till the end

I love my solitude but I was meant to be a lover

Now she goes crying
Please don't stop trying
Life gets hard when the night gets dark
But don't stop loving

And your heart will bring
What you've been missing
A romance straight out of a fairy movie
So don't stop dreaming

k. wildside




I want to bite
In a thick bright colored love

Cause mine only taste like marshmellow and black licorice

Could you be my forbidden bliss

I think she loves it so much
To see anyone new is old
And to surrender to her gut
Letting her past stay deep blue cold

It makes her feel at home
To meet brand new ghosts
They tell the same story of hope
With an empty future in their moans

But she would love to wake up
With brand new eyes

Without any signs
Of her dear old cries

And after that moment of trust
The chase was over

She listened to heart
And silence
She listened to her head
For guidance

But she was never lost
It's always been within her

She decided to lit a candle
Right across her heart
To mourn a ground that was unstable
And hoping for a fire to start

The flame just flirted around
Looking to spark another lie
But with no desires left to be found
She realized with her smile

She was still safe and sound

k. wildside

She has blood at the tip of her tongue
From the words she chewed up
Thinking she was wrong
Taught to keep her mouth shut

So she learned to kill with her eyes
When the sounds would choke
Her sight would cut open wide
To pour out the antidote

She drew a moon on her finger

Because she is bound to the night
It's when she strips off her mind
To let her smile feels alive

The dark light calls her its child
She worships it's shadow
Because it never let her go

She has her heart on the moon in the sky

k. wildside

You voice is my hospital

He gave her his chocolate heart
Filled with desires that could tear him apart

She handpicked to her needs
The pieces thinking they were the keys

With only one left in the box
She turned her back and started to walk

She left feeling empty to her stomach
He said he was only full of regrets

k. wildside

All she wanted to play was cat and mouse
In her four dark blue walls house
Making him run breathless
Until his heart spillled into a mess

Wanted him to crawl and chase
Only made his feelings pace
This house wasn't love made
As he only felt like a bait

She trapped him in her cold
Until the games grew old

Until he cracked too much to play with

Her laughs and smiles were the matches
And her hands the artist
She folded it as she wished
A self portrait colored from ashes

k. wildside

Holes and dead lines were scarred into it
But she couldn't care less
Hers was just as distressed
She said with a kiss

We were fragile from the start
But rebelled

Against our paper hearts

She could read me from her lips
And draw my heart in a kiss
Her eyes would never leave my mind
And her laugh could stop the time

Any of my words are hers
And the lines of my mouth are blurred
She could see through my desire
And make me sound like a lover

But everything is a lust
As I'm left alone in the dust

k. wildside

She teared it out of herself
And held it high above her head
Poored it down inside his tight throat
Only to let him know and soaked

She made him drink
Until he understood
And it changed him
Like nothing ever could
Crystalized down his
Deep blue heart
And opened an ocean
For her to start a war

You wet my eyes
When I wanted you
To drench my heart

Take me back to when we met
When we weren't so far
Apart

k. wildside

Why can't the sun
Be late in the morning

Like everytime you are
Beside me sleeping

I am so far away
In my head
In my thoughts
On my bed

I'll send you a postcard
Of the sunrise
Since you kept me up all night

k. wildside

Her answer was to become heartless
And as cold as december
She decided to be careless
So she couldn't get hurt

He is determined to show her
That his heart is the safest
Where no tears or fear can enter
But only true love lives in his chest

She looked through his smile
And saw her favourite dream
Love was there and keen
And she couldn't understand why

He looked through her eyes
And saw his worst nightmare
Fear was left alone in there
And he couldn't understand why

They went their separate ways
Never answered
Never fulfilled
But forever hurt

The tale of two young lovers

k. wildside

She wanted him alive
Giving just enough to breathe
Just enough to make it seems
She wanted him to thrive

He was scared it was a lie
The doubt filled his blood
But the demon won against the odds
He was ready to cry

But she carved him a smile

We ran out of tomorrows
But I will live on the yesterdays
We shared together

Until they fade away

Until they follow you

Let me know
If you have an empty space

I could make myself at home

I could paint your heart happy
And we could

Live romantically

I know
If you open yourself to me

I will find the golden ticket
I have been looking for

k. wildside

123

I built a bridge
Just for us two

So we can lock our lips

And wish upon cupid

You should be soaking in colors

But you'd rather be drowning
In black and white

k. wildside

I lost my head
Somewhere around your chest

Or into your arms

Could you bring it back
If the weight is too much

It's the possibilities
Of all the tomorrows
In your company

That makes the distance
Irrelevant
To our story

k. wildside

I don't know how to call it
But it sure knows our names

And how to make us trip
Into each other's arms

You live in such a sadness
It could eat you up

But you're acting so colorful
With your head up

You want them to see you strong

But there's nothing wrong
With who you are

k. wildside

You broke into mine
Slipped in between the tiny little pieces
Seeing all the tiny little places
That's been hurt

But you talked them back together

You will need to fill up a jar
For I have been hurt and scarred

Fill it up with time
Kind words
Kisses and signs

You will be there for a while

And once it reaches bliss

I will whisper my love on your lips

k. wildside

It is only a half goodbye
Since my heart
Swallowed the other

I refuse to take my eyes
Off of the pages
Where we were lovers

So I heard the saying
Wild hearts can't be broken
They can't
In fact

They get wilder
And harder and harder
To get closer

k. wildside

Yesterday was so different
I was seeing from my own eyes

Now there's a little bit of you
Everywhere I see

Like a filter
Coloring inside the lines

h o n e y t r a p

Listen

Love is filled with opportunities equally
bad and beautiful. Every relationship counts,
even when they feel like a honeytrap.
Remember the honey, those sweet moments
where you felt loved and cared for,
or you felt like you were something worth fighting for,
those moments, no matter how long,
will outlived those when you felt
trapped and cheated on and used.
They will carry you and will teach you
better on what love really is.
I am not saying it will bring you closer
to a love that will last forever,
but it will bring you a closer look
at what is happiness, romance and respect
in a relationship, because while love
might not always last forever
it should at least be
dreamy and peaceful and taste like honey.